M000233808

The Antichrist

Vladimir Soloviev

Soloviev, a Russian mystic and philosopher, wrote the Antichrist as a prophecy of the end of this century. It contains insights surprisingly relevant to understanding the currents in the world today.

R; RP 1982; 60pp; 5½″ x 8½″
0-86315-501-4; sb; **$6.95**

The Antichrist

Vladimir Soloviev

The Antichrist

Floris Classics

Translated by W J Barnes and H H Haynes

This short narrative is from the last of three 'Conversations'
which comprise *War and Christianity,* first published in Russian in
1900. First published in English by Constable & Co. Ltd. in 1915.

This edition published by Floris Books, Edinburgh in 1982

ISBN 0-86315-501-4

Printed in Great Britain
by Billing & Sons, Worcester

Contents

Introduction by Adam Bittleston   11

The Antichrist   17

Introduction

Introduction

Vladimir Soloviev (1853-1901) was one of the greatest Russian thinkers and a thinker of a very special kind. His ideas are warm and so filled with spiritual light that they constantly approach the threshold of prophetic vision. On certain great occasions in his life the heavens opened for him. Three times he saw the Virgin Sophia and received guidance from her. The first time was when as a boy of nine he attended the Orthodox liturgy on Ascension Day. The second was in the Reading Room of the British Museum. The third was in the desert in Egypt.

He taught and wrote always with the certainty that Wisdom is One and is a living, loving being. He was deeply concerned about the divisions within Christianity but reached the conviction that unity could not be achieved by external means, or through the abandonment by Orthodoxy, Roman Catholicism or Protestantism of their great characteristic qualities. Each should prepare to face a future in which

11

Christians could grow to maturity and mutual love through great trials.

Late in his life, he wrote the dialogue 'War and Christianity' of which the story reprinted here forms the conclusion. The discussion had been on matters of principle: the Christian attitude to conflict, social problems and so on. Eventually, one of the participants launches out into what can be taken as a parable but is much more. Soloviev sees that Christians may be tempted to forsake the essential mysteries of their faith under the pressure of an adversary who will wear a very attractive and apparently benevolent disguise. It will not be easy to escape from the impression that the external, visible and measurable world is the only reality, and that what appears best for men in this world is really the best or even the only reasonable course to take. Those who recognize in man potential organs of spiritual perception of a higher reality, and who come to regard the right development of these organs as in accordance with the will of Christ, can expect to have to face at some time crushing indifference or bitter hostility, or an ingenious combination of the two.

Soloviev felt in advance a good deal of the

meaning of the twentieth century, its dangers and its inner triumphs. And he saw that Christianity, to be worthy of its mission in this century, would have to struggle through to a new level of understanding.

Adam Bittleston

The Antichrist

MR. Z. (*reads*).—The twentieth century after the birth of Christ was the period of the last great wars, civil dissension and revolutions. The very greatest of foreign wars had as its remote cause, the intellectual movement of Pan-mongolism which arose in Japan towards the end of the nineteenth century. The imitative Japanese, with astonishing rapidity and success copied the material forms of European culture and adopted certain European ideas of a lower order. Having learned from newspapers and historical text-books about the existence in the West of Pan-hellenism, Pan-germanism, Pan-slavism, Pan-islamism, they proclaimed the great idea of Pan-mongolism, which was the gathering into one, under their leadership, of all the peoples of Eastern Asia with the object of making a resolute struggle against foreigners, that is to say, Europeans. Taking advantage of the fact that Europe was engaged in a final and decisive struggle with the Moslem world in the beginning of the twentieth century, they began the realisation of a great plan—first, the occupation of Korea, then that of Peking, where, with the help of the progressive party in China they would depose the ancient Manchurian dynasty and put the Japanese in its place. The Chinese Conservatives soon came to an agreement with them. They saw that of two evils it was better to choose the lesser and therefore, blood being thicker than water, they necessarily chose their brothers the Japanese.

17

The government of China had not the power to hold its ground and would have unavoidably become subject either to the Europeans or to the Japanese. But it was clear that the Japanese sovereignty, abolishing the external forms of Chinese dominion which seemed eminently trivial, would not affect the intimate foundations of national life, whilst on the other hand the predominance of the European powers, who supported, for political reasons, the Christian missionaries, would threaten the deepest spiritual foundations of China. The former national hatred of the Chinese for the Japanese had arisen at a time when neither the one nor the other had known Europeans, in the presence of whom this enmity of two related peoples became mere civil dissension, and lost any significance. Europeans were entirely foreigners, merely enemies, and their domination could in no way be flattering to race pride, whilst in the hands of Japan, the Chinese saw the delightful lure of Pan-mongolism, which, moreover, in their eyes did away with the sad inevitability of European influence. " You see, O obstinate brothers," said the Japanese, " that we take the arms of the Western dogs, not from any infatuation for them, but simply to beat them with their own weapons. If you join us and accept our practical guidance we shall not only quickly drive the white devils out of our Asia, but we shall fight them in their own countries and found a real middle kingdom over the whole world. You are right in your national pride and contempt of Europeans, but it is vain to nourish these feelings on dreams alone without intelligent activity. In this we have surpassed you and we must show you the way of our common welfare. Otherwise, see for yourselves what your policy of self-assurance and distrust of us, your natural friends and defenders, has given you: Russia and England, Germany and France have almost shared you between them, leaving you nothing, and all your tigerish plots show only the weak end of a serpent's tail." Reasonable Chinamen found this sound, and the Japanese dynasty pronounced it well founded. Its first care, of course, was the creation of a powerful army and navy. A great part of the fighting forces of Japan was brought to China, where it composed the staff of an enormous new army. Japanese officers speaking Chinese acted as instructors far more successfully than the Europeans who had been dismissed, and in the countless populations of China, Manchuria, Mongolia and Tibet was found a sufficiency of excellent military material. Already the first Chinese Emperor of the Japanese dynasty was able to make a successful trial of the arms of the revived empire, driving out the French from Tonkin and Siam, the English from Burma, and including in the Middle Empire all of Indo-China. His heir, Chinese on his mother's side, thus uniting in himself both the cunning and elasticity of the Chinese with the energy, mobility and enterprise of the Japanese, mobilised in Chinese Turkestan an army of four millions, and at the time that the Tsun-li-Yamin confidently informed the Russian Ambassador that this force was intended for the conquest of India, the Emperor appears in our Central Asia, and having collected there all the inhabitants, moves swiftly across the Urals and swamps with his armies all Eastern and Central Russia, whilst the Russian forces, hastily mobilised in various parts, hurry from Poland, from Lithuania, from Kiev, Volhynia, Petersburg and Finland. Owing to the absence of a prearranged plan of campaign and the enormous numerical superiority of the enemy, the fighting qualities of the Russian forces allow them only to perish with honour. The swiftness of the invasion left no time for the necessary concentration, and army corps after army corps was exterminated in hard and hopeless conflicts. The Mongols did not come off cheaply, but they easily replaced their losses, having control of all the Asiatic railways, while a Russian army of two hundred thousand, for a long time concentrated on the Manchurian frontier, made an unsuccessful attempt to invade a well-defended China. Having left a part of his forces in Russia to prevent the forming of new armies, and also for the pursuit of guerilla bands which had increased in number, the Emperor with three armies crossed the German frontier. Here they had succeeded in making preparations, and one of the Mongol armies was annihilated. At this time the party of a belated *revanche* was in power in France and a million hostile bayonets quickly appeared at the Germans' back. Having fallen between the anvil and the hammer, the German army was forced to accept honourable conditions of surrender proposed by the Emperor. The jubilant French fraternising with the yellow faces were scattered throughout Germany, and soon lost every appearance of military discipline. The Emperor commanded his soldiers to kill the more unnecessary of his allies, which was accomplished with Chinese accuracy. In Paris an uprising of working men *sans patrie* took place, and the capital of western culture opened its gates to the Conqueror of the East. Having satisfied his curiosity, the Emperor set out for Boulogne, where, under cover of the fleet which had come from the Pacific, he got ready transports to convey his army to Great Britain. But he was in need of money, and the English bought their freedom for a milliard pounds. For a year all the European Powers acknowledged themselves vassals of the Emperor, who, having left a sufficient army of occupation in Europe, returned to the East, where he began preparations for a naval expedition against America and Australia. For half a century Europe lay under the Mongol yoke. In the domain of thought this epoch was remarkable for a general blending and mutual interchange of European and Eastern ideas, a repetition *en grand* of the ancient Alexandrian syncritism. In the practical domain of life, three phenomena became in the highest degree characteristic : the large influx into Europe of Chinese and Japanese labour, and in consequence of this the violent embitterment of the social-economic question ; the series of palliative attempts to solve this question, which were prolonged on the part of the governing classes ; and the increasing international activity of secret social organisations which resulted in a widespread European plot to drive out the Mongols and to re-establish the independence of Europe. This colossal plot, into which the local national governments entered so far as they were able, being under the control of the Imperial viceroys, was prepared in a masterly and succeeded in a brilliant manner. At an appointed time began the slaughter of the Mongol soldiers and the murder and expulsion of the workmen. In all places secret staffs of the European army appeared, and a general mobilisation took place according to a long-prepared and circumstantial plan. The new Emperor, the grandson of the great Conqueror, hastened from China to Russia, but here his numberless hordes were annihilated by the all-European army. Their scattered remnants returned to the depths of Asia, and Europe became free. If the half century of subjugation to the Asiatic barbarians was the result of the disunion of the Powers, who thought only of their separate national interests, a great and glorious liberation was attained by the international organisation of the united forces of all the peoples of Europe.

As a natural consequence of this obvious fact it followed that the old traditional order of divided nations everywhere lost its significance, and almost everywhere the last traces of monarchical institutions disappeared. Europe in the twenty-first century presented a union of more or less democratic States—the United States of Europe. The progress of external culture, somewhat retarded by the Mongol invasion and war of liberation, again

went forward. Matters of internal consciousness—
questions of life and death, of the last judgment, of
the world and of mankind, complicated and confused
by a multitude of new physiological and psycho-
logical investigations and discoveries remained as
formerly, insoluble. Only one important negative
result was made clear—the absolute fall of theoretical
materialism. The representation of the universe as
a system of floating atoms, and of life as the result
of a mechanical agglomeration of minute alterations
of matter—such a statement no longer satisfied even
one thinking being. Mankind had for ever outgrown
this stage of philosophical youthfulness. But it was
clear on the other hand that it had also outgrown
the youthful capacity of a simple and unconscious
belief. The idea that God created the universe out
of nothing, etc., ceased to be taught even in the
primary schools. A certain general and higher level
of representing such matters had been worked out,
below which no dogmatism could fall. And if the
vast majority of thinking people remained entirely
unbelievers, the few who believed became of necessity
" thinkers," fulfilling the instructions of the apostle :
be children at heart but not in mind.

There was at this time among the few people
believing in spiritual things a remarkable man—
called by many a superman—who was, however,
as far from being intellectual as from being a child
at heart. He was still young, but, thanks to his
great talent, at thirty-three years of age was widely
proclaimed as a great thinker, writer, and social
worker. Being conscious within himself of great

spiritual power he had been always a convinced spiritualist, and his clear understanding always showed him the truth of that in which one must believe—Good, God, the Messiah. In these he *believed*, but he *loved only himself*. He believed in God, but, in the depths of his soul, he involuntarily and unconsciously preferred himself to Him. He believed in Good, but the All Seeing Eye of the Eternal knew that this man bowed before the power of evil when it offered him a bribe—not by the snare of the senses and lower passions, nor even by the superior attraction of power, but through his immeasurable self-love alone. Besides, this self-love was neither an unconscious instinct nor a foolish pretence. In view of his exceptional talent, his beauty, nobility of character, his supreme display of continence, his disinterestedness, and his active beneficence, it seemed that his enormous self-love was justifiable, and worthy of a great spiritualist, ascetic, and philanthropist. Was he to blame ?—a man so plenteously endowed with divine gifts that he saw in them special signs of an exceptional affection from heaven for himself, and he counted himself as second to God in his origin as the only son of God. In a word, he avowed that he was, in truth, Christ. But this consciousness of his supermerit, in effect, defined itself in him not as any moral obligation of his towards God and the world, but as his right and prerogative to be before others, and, more than all, before Christ. He had no fundamental enmity towards Jesus. He recognised His Messianic significance and merit, and he really saw in Him his own august predecessor. The moral grandeur and absolute oneness of Christ were not understood by a mind clouded by self-love. He argued thus : " Christ came before me ; I appeared next, but that which appears later in time is, in reality, first. I shall come last at the end of history exactly because I am the absolute and final saviour. The first Christ is my forerunner. His mission was to prepare and make ready for my appearance." In this sense the great man of the twenty-first century applied to himself all that was said in the Gospel about the Second Advent, proclaiming that this advent is not a return of the same Christ but a substitution of the previous Christ which is final, that is, he himself.

On this point the coming man does not yet offer much that is characteristic or original. He regards his relation to Christ in the same way as did, for instance, Mahomet, an upright man, whom it is impossible to accuse of any evil design.

The self-loving preference of himself to Christ was justified by this man with such an argument as follows : " Christ, preaching and proclaiming moral welfare, was the reformer of humanity, but I am called to be benefactor of humanity in part reformed, in part unreformed. I shall give to everyone all that is necessary for him. Christ as a moralist divided all people into good and bad ; I shall unite them by blessings which are necessary both to the good and the bad. I shall be the real representative of that God who causes the sun to shine upon the good and the bad, and the rain to fall upon the just and unjust. Christ brought a sword; I shall bring peace. He threatened the earth with a dreadful last judgment. But I shall be the final judge, and my judgment will not be a judgment of right only, but of mercy. There will be justice in my judgment; not a justice of reward, but a distributive justice. I shall make a distinction for all, and to each one I shall give what is needful for him."

And behold, in this beautiful frame of mind he awaits some clear, divine call for a new salvation of humanity; for some clear and striking evidence that he is the eldest and beloved firstborn Son of God. He awaits and nourishes his being with the consciousness of his superhuman beneficence and abilities—and this, as it has been said, is a man of irreproachable morality and unusual talent.

The proud and just man waits for the highest sanction in order to begin his salvation of humanity —but he waits in vain. He has passed his thirtieth year and still another three years go by. Suddenly the thought flashes into his mind and pierces to the depths of his brain with a burning shudder, " But if? if it is not I, but that other—the Galilean. If He is not my forerunner, but the real first and last? But He must be *alive*—where is He? . . . If He came to me now and here . . . What shall I say to Him? I must bend low before Him, as the very simplest Christian, and as a Russian mouzhik murmur stupidly, ' Lord Jesus Christ, have mercy upon me a sinner,' or, like an old Polish woman, prostrate myself before Him, flat on the ground. I, the brilliant genius, the superman!

No, never ! " And in the place of the former reasonable and cold respect for God and Christ there is born and grows up in his heart, at first a sort of horror and then a burning envy and fury which seizes and contracts all his being, a hatred which fills his soul. " It is I, and not He. He is not alive and will not be. He has not, He has not risen ! He is rotting in the grave, rotting as the lost . . ." With foaming mouth and convulsive bounds.he rushed from the house and the garden, and in the heavy, black night ran along the path on the cliffs. His fury had abated and a despair, hard and heavy as the cliff, gloomy as the night, had taken its place. He stopped near a perpendicular break in the cliff and listened to the troubled noise of the water among the stones far below him. An unbearable sorrow crushed his heart. Suddenly there was a movement within him. " Shall I call upon Him—shall I ask Him what to do ? " And in the midst of the darkness appeared a gentle and sad image. " He pities me ! no, never ! He is not risen, He is not risen ! " And he flung himself away from the brink. But something as elastic as a waterspout carried him up in the air, and he felt a vibration as from an electric current when some power hurled him back. For an instant he lost consciousness, and when he regained his senses he found himself kneeling a few steps away from the edge of the cliff. Before him was the outline of a figure, bright with a phosphorescent misty radiance, whose eyes with unbearably sharp brilliancy pierced his soul.

He saw these two piercing eyes and heard,

proceeding neither from within nor from without, a strange voice, dull, as if smothered, and, at the same time, precise and entirely soulless, as if it came from a gramophone. This voice said to him : " My well-beloved son, all my affection is in thee. Why hast thou sought me ? Why honour that other, the wicked One and His Father. I am god and thy father. The other—a beggar and crucified One—is a stranger to me and to thee. I have no other son but thee. Thou, my only, only begotten, equal to me. I love thee and ask nothing of thee. Thou art so beautiful, great and powerful. Act in thine own name, not in mine. I do not envy thee ; I love thee. I am in need of nothing from thee. He, whom thou didst deem a god, demanded of His Son obedience and boundless subservience, even to the death of the cross, and He was unable to help Him on the cross. I require nothing of thee, and I shall help thee. For thine own sake and the sake of thy special worthiness and superiority and my pure, disinterested love to thee, I shall help thee. Receive my spirit. As, formerly, my spirit brought thee forth in beauty, so now let it beget thee in strength." At these words of the unknown the lips of the superman parted wide, two piercing eyes approached closely to his face, and he felt as if a sharp, icy current was entering into him, filling all his being. Moreover, he felt a marvellous strength, daring, lightness and ecstasy. At the same instant the shining countenance and the two piercing eyes suddenly disappeared, and something lifted the superman from earth and dropped him immediately in his garden near the door of his house.

On the following day not only the visitors of the
great man, but even his servants, were amazed at
his inspired appearance. But they would have been
still more astonished if they had been able to see
with what supernatural swiftness and easiness he,
having locked himself up in his own study, wrote
his remarkable work under the title of " The Open
Way to Universal Peace and Prosperity."

The previous books and general activities of the
superman had met with severe critics, although they
were for the most part especially religious people,
and for that reason had no authority of any kind—
of course, I am speaking of the time of the coming
of Antichrist—so that not many listened to them
when they pointed out, in everything that the
" coming man " wrote and said, the signs of an
absolutely exceptional, intense self-love and conceit,
with the absence of true simplicity, rectitude and
zeal.

But by his new work he attracted to himself
even some of his former critics and opponents.
This book, written after the adventure on the cliff,
showed in him an unprecedented power of genius.
It was something all-embracing and calculated to
reconcile all dispute. In it was united a noble
reverence for ancient traditions and symbols, with
a broad and daring radicalism in social-political
demands and requirements ; a boundless freedom
of thought with the deepest understanding of
all mysticism, unconditional individualism, with a
burning zeal for the common good, the most exalted
idealism in guiding principles, with the complete

definiteness and vitality of practical solutions.
And all of it was united and connected with such
genius and art that it was easy for every one-sided
thinker and worker to see and accept the whole, even
from his personal angle of vision, in no way sacri-
ficing truth itself, not magnifying it effectively over
his "Ego," not disclaiming the practicability of
his one-sidedness nor correcting the faults of his
outlook and aims, nor yet completing their short-
comings. This wonderful book was at once translated into all the languages of the civilised—and
some of the uncivilised—nations. A thousand
newspapers in all parts of the world were filled for
a whole year with editorial articles and with the
raptures of the critics. Cheap editions, with por-
traits of the author, were sold in millions of copies,
and the whole of the cultured world—which at that
period comprised almost the whole earth—was filled
with the fame of the incomparable great and only
one ! No one made any objections to this book—
it seemed to each the revelation of entire truth. In
it such full justice was done to all the past, all
the present was estimated so dispassionately and
broadly, and the best future was so clearly and
realistically described, that everyone said: " Here
is the very thing I need ; this is the ideal which is
not Utopian ; this is a project which is not chimeri-
cal." And the wonderful author not only attracted
everyone, but he was *welcome* to each, thus fulfilling
the words of Christ :

" I am come in My Father's name and ye receive
Me not ; if another shall come in his own name—him

ye will receive." Of course, for the latter to be received he must be welcome.

It is true, some pious people, while warmly praising the book, began to ask why Christ was not once mentioned in it ; but other Christians replied, " God be praised ! Already, in past centuries, all holy things have been sufficiently soiled by every sort of unacknowledged zealot, and now a deeply religious writer must be very guarded. And if the contents of a book are impregnated with the truly Christian spirit of effective love and universal benevolence, what is there left to wish for ?" With this all agreed. Soon after the appearance of " The Open Way," which made its author the most popular of all the people who had lived in the world, the international constitutional assembly of the Union of European States was to meet. This Union, founded after the series of domestic and foreign wars which were connected with the throwing off of the Mongol yoke, and which considerably changed the map of Europe, was faced with the immediate danger of a collision—not between the nations, but between political and social parties. The principal directors of general European policy belonging to the powerful society of Freemasons felt the lack of a common executive authority. European unity, which had been attained with such difficulty, was ready at any moment to fall to pieces. The federated council, or universal committee (*comité permanent universel*), was not in harmony, since not all the places were occupied by real Masons devoted to the matter. Independent members of the committee entered into a separate agreement among themselves, and the matter threatened to cause a new war. Then the "devoted ones" resolved to institute a personal executive authority of one man, with full and sufficient powers. The principal candidate was a member of the Order, "the coming man."

He was the only person with a great world-wide reputation. Being by profession a clever officer of artillery, and by his possessions a large capitalist, he had friendly relations everywhere in financial and military circles. In other and less enlightened times the fact that his origin was obscured by a heavy mist of the unknown would have militated against him. His mother, a person of indulgent conduct, was well known in both hemispheres, but too many different people had good reason to believe themselves his father. These circumstances naturally could not have any significance in a century so much in the van, that even to him it appeared to be the last. The "coming man" was elected almost unanimously as life president of the United States of Europe. When he appeared in the Tribune, in all the glory of his superhuman youthful beauty and power, and in an inspired discourse of great eloquence expounded his universal programme, the assembly, enchanted and carried away, decided, in a burst of enthusiasm and without voting, to pay him the highest honour by electing him as Roman Emperor. The Congress was closed amid the greatest rejoicing, and the great man who had been chosen issued a manifesto which began thus:

" Peoples of the earth, my peace I give to you,"
and ending with the words, " Peoples of the earth !
The promises have been performed. An eternal,
universal peace has been secured. Every attempt
to destroy it will meet with invincible resistance.
For, from henceforth, there is one central authority
on earth, which is stronger than all other powers
taken separately and together. This invincible,
all-subduing authority, with all its power, belongs
to me, as chosen autocratic Emperor of Europe.
International law has, at last, a sanction hitherto
unattained by it. From henceforth no power will
dare to say ' War ' when I say it is ' Peace.' Peoples
of the earth, peace be to you! " This manifesto
produced the desired effect. Everywhere outside
Europe, especially in America, strong imperialistic
parties were formed which forced their governments,
upon various conditions, to join the United States of
Europe under the supreme power of the Roman
Emperor. There still remained independent tribes
and smaller powers somewhere in Asia and Africa.
The Emperor, with a small army, but one chosen
from Russian, German, Polish, Hungarian and
Turkish regiments, accomplished a march from
Eastern Asia to Morocco, and without great blood-
shed brought into subjection all who were dis-
obedient. He established viceroys in all the
countries of both hemispheres, men of European education and native magnates devoted to
himself. The population of all pagan countries was
dumbfounded, but at the same time enchanted,
and proclaimed him a great god. In one year, in a

real and accurate sense, he founded a universal mon-
archy. All tendencies to war were eradicated. The
League of Universal Peace met for the last time,
and having published an enthusiastic panegyric on
the great peace maker, abolished itself as unnecessary. In the second year of his reign the Roman
and Universal Emperor issued a new manifesto.
" Peoples of the earth, I promised you peace and I
have given it you. But peace is beautiful only
when coupled with prosperity. He who in time of
peace is threatened with the misfortune of poverty,
does not find peace a joy. Now, let all who are
cold and hungry come to me, so that I may warm
them and feed them.' Afterwards he announced
a simple and all-embracing social reform which,
already stated in his book, had there captivated all
noble and sober minds. At present, thanks to the
concentration in his hands of the world's finance and
of a colossal amount of landed property, he was able
to realise this reform according to the wishes of the
poor, and without sensibly offending the rich. Everyone began to receive in proportion to his ability,
and every ability according to its labour and merit. '

The new lord of the earth was, before all things,
a tender-hearted philanthropist, and not only a
philanthropist but a *philosopher*. He himself was
a vegetarian. He forbad vivisection, and instituted
a strict watch over slaughter-houses. The society
for the protection of animals was encouraged by
him in every way. But more important than all
these details was the solid establishment among all
mankind of the most fundamental equality—*an*

equality of general repletion. This was accomplished in the second year of his reign. The social-political question was definitely settled. But if repletion be the first interest of hungry people, such people, when once replete, want something more. Even animals, when replete, usually want not only to sleep, but to play. Much more than they, do human beings, who at all times, *post panem*, have demanded *circenses*.

The Emperor-superman understood what was necessary for his people. At this time a great magician from distant Orient came to him in Rome wrapped in a thick cloud of strange happenings and curious tales. It was generally believed among the Neo-Buddhists that he was of divine origin—a son of the sun god Surga and of a water nymph.

This magician, Apollyon by name, was a man undoubtedly talented, half Asiatic, half European, a Catholic bishop *in partibus infidelium*, who, while he was to an astonishing degree in possession of the latest results of Western science and of its technical application, also united with this the knowledge of all that is really sound and significant in the traditional mysticism of the Orient and the skill to make use of it. The results of such a combination were astounding. Apollyon had attained, amongst other things, the skill at once, half scientific, half magical, of attracting and directing atmospheric electricity, and told the people *he brought down fire from heaven*. For the rest, while striking the imagination of the crowd by various unheard-of wonders, he had not up to now made ill use of his power for any personal aims. So this man came to the great Emperor and bowing before him as before a true son of God, declared that in the secret books of the East he had found direct prophecies about him, the Emperor, as the last saviour and universal judge, and placed himself and his art at his service. The Emperor, enchanted with him, received him as a gift from heaven, and after conferring upon him the highest titles, refused henceforth to be parted from him. The peoples of the earth, loaded with the benefits of their lord, were to have, besides general peace and repletion, the possibility, moreover, of constant enjoyment of the most varied and unexpected wonders and phenomena. So ended the third year of the superman's reign.

After the happy solution of the political and social questions, the religious question arose. It was raised by the Emperor himself, particularly in its relation to Christianity. At this time Christianity found itself in the following position. In face of a very considerable diminution in the number of its members—there were not more than 45,000,000 Christians left in all the world—morally it had pulled itself up and braced itself and had gained in quality what it had lost in quantity. There were no longer numbered among Christians any people who were not concerned with some Christian spiritual interest. The various confessions of faith diminished proportionately in numbers, and consequently they preserved approximately their former numerical relation. As to their mutual feelings, although enmity had not given place to complete reconciliation yet it was notably softened and opposition lost

its sharpness. The Papacy had already for some
time been driven out of Rome, and after many
wanderings had found an asylum in Petersburg, on
condition that it refrained from propaganda both in
that town and in the country. In Russia it became
noticeably simpler. While not changing the essentially necessary composition of its college and
officers, it was obliged to spiritualise the character
of its activities and also to reduce to a minimum its
magnificent ritual and ceremonial. Many strange
and enticing customs, although not formally
abolished, went of themselves out of use. In all
other countries, especially in North America, the
Catholic hierarchy had many representatives, firm in
will, of indomitable energy and of independent
position, who, more strongly than ever, insisted on
the unity of the Catholic Church, and preserved for
her her international and cosmopolitan importance.
As to Protestantism, at the head of which Germany
continued to stand—especially after the reunion of
a considerable part of the Anglican Church with
Catholicism—it purged itself of its extreme negative
tendencies, and the supporters of those tendencies
openly descended to religious indifference and
unbelief. In the Evangelical churches there remained only sincere believers, at whose head stood
persons who combined a wide knowledge with a deep
religious consciousness, and who tried with all the
more effort to revive in themselves a living image
of the ancient and original Christianity. Now that
political events had changed the official position
of the Church, Russian Orthodoxy, although it

had lost many of its former nominal members, yet experienced the joy of union with the best part of the Old Believers, and even with many sects of a definitely religious tendency. This revivified Church, though it did not grow in numbers, did grow in spiritual power, and this power it showed especially in its domestic struggle with the extreme sects which had increased amongst the people and in society, sects which were not lacking in the demoniac and satanic element.

During the first two years of the new reign the Christians, frightened and depressed by the series of revolutions and wars that had gone before, respected the new ruler and his peaceful reforms, some from a well-disposed expectation, others with absolute sympathy and burning enthusiasm. But with the appearance of the great magician in the third year, serious apprehensions and antipathies began to arise amongst many of the Orthodox, Catholics and Evangelicals. The evangelistic and apostolic texts, which spoke of the prince of this world and Antichrist, began to be read with more attention and discussed with animation. From certain indications the Emperor suspected a gathering storm and resolved to clear up the matter quickly. In the beginning of the fourth year of his reign he issued a manifesto to all his faithful Christians, without distinction of creed, inviting them to choose or designate a representative, with full powers for a general council under his presidency. His residence at this time had been changed from Rome to Jerusalem. Palestine was then an autonomous State inhabited and governed principally by Jews. Jerusalem was a free and had been made an imperial city. The Christian holy places had remained inviolate, but upon the spacious platform of Kharam-esh-Sherif, from Berket-Israin and the present barracks on one side to the mosque of El-Ak and "Solomon's Stables" on the other, was erected an enormous edifice including, besides the two ancient small mosques, a spacious "imperial" temple for the union of all cults, and two magnificent imperial palaces with libraries, museums and special apartments for magical experiments and practices. In this half-temple, half-palace, the general council was to be opened on the 14th of September. Since the Evangelical religion had no priesthood in the true sense, the Catholic and Orthodox hierarchy resolved agreeably to the wish of the Emperor, and in order to give a certain homogeneity to the representatives of all forms of Christianity, to allow a certain number of laymen, well known for their piety and devoted to the interests of the Church, to have a part in the council. Once laymen were allowed it was impossible to exclude the lower clergy, both black and white. In this way the number of members of the council exceeded three thousand, and about half a million of Christian pilgrims deluged Jerusalem and Palestine. Among the members of the council there were three who especially stood out. The first was Pope Peter II., by right at the head of the Catholic part of the council. His predecessor had died on the way to the council, and a conclave having been convened at Damascus, Cardinal

Simone Barione was unanimously elected and took the name of Peter. He was of humble origin, came from the Neapolitan district, and had become known as a preacher of the Carmelite Order who rendered great service in the struggle against a Satanist sect which was growing in strength in Petersburg and the surrounding country, and which had led astray not only Orthodox but Catholics. Made Archbishop of Mogilef and then cardinal, he was early marked out for the tiara. He was a man of fifty years of age, of middle height and robust constitution, red-faced, with a hooked nose and thick eyebrows. Impetuous and full of ardour, he spoke fervently with bold · gestures, and attracted his auditors more than he persuaded them. The new Pope expressed both distrust and dislike of the universal sovereign; especially was this the case as the late Pope, when leaving for the council, had yielded to the insistence of the Emperor and appointed as a cardinal the imperial chancellor and universal magician, the esoteric Bishop Apollyon, whom Peter considered a doubtful Catholic but undoubted impostor. The actual, though unofficial, leader of the Orthodox was the venerable John, very well known among the Russian people. Although he was officially considered a bishop " in retirement," he did not live in any monastery, but constantly travelled in all directions. There were various legends about him. Some believed that he was Fedor Kouzmich brought back to life, namely, the Emperor Alexander I., who had been born about three centuries before that time. Others went farther and affirmed that he was the Apostle St. John the Divine, who, never having died, now appeared openly in the latter days. He himself said nothing about his origin or youth. He was now very old, but hale and hearty, with yellowish, even greenish white curls and beard, tall, thin in body, with full, rosy cheeks and bright, sparkling eyes, sympathetic both in the expression of his face and in his conversation. He was always dressed in a white cassock and cloak. At the head of the Evangelical members of the council stood the learned German theologian Professor Ernst Pauli. He was a dried-up, little old man of medium height, with an enormous brow, sharp nose and clean-shaven chin. His eyes were distinguished by a certain ferociously kind-hearted look. He constantly rubbed his hands, shook his head, twitched his eyebrows in a strange way and stuck out his lips, while at the same time with flashing eyes he gruffly uttered broken sounds : So ! nun ! ja ! so also ! He was dressed solemnly —with a white tie and long pastor's coat, and wore the badges of certain Orders.

The opening of the council was inspiring. Two-thirds of the enormous temple consecrated to the " union of all cults " was furnished with benches and other seats for the members of the council, the remaining third was occupied by a high daïs, on which behind the imperial throne and another, lower down, for the great magician—who was at the same time cardinal and imperial chancellor—there were rows of armchairs for the ministers, courtiers and secretaries of state, and on one side a still further line of armchairs, the use of which was unknown.

In the choir was an orchestra and, on a neighbouring platform, two regiments of the guards were drawn up and a battery for triumphant salvos. The members of the council had already celebrated religious services in their various churches, and the opening of the council was to be entirely secular. When the Emperor entered, accompanied by the great magician and his suite, the orchestra played the "March of United Humanity," which served as the imperial international hymn, and all the members of the council arose, and waving their hats shouted three times, " Vivat ! Hurrah ! Hoch ! " The Emperor, standing by the throne, stretching forth his hand with majestic benevolence, said in a resonant and pleasing voice : " Christians of all cults ! My well-beloved subjects and brethren ! From the beginning of my reign, which the Most High has blessed with such wonderful and note-worthy deeds, not once have I had cause to be dis-pleased with you; you have always fulfilled your duty according to your belief and conscience. This con-cerns me but little. My sincere love for you, dear brothers, longs for some return. I desire that you, not through any feeling of duty, but through a feel-ing of zealous love, should recognise me as your true guide in every matter which has been undertaken for the welfare of humanity. But, besides that which I am doing for everyone, I should like to show you special favour. Christians ! what can I do to make you happy ? What shall I give you, not as my subjects, but as fellow-believers, as my brethren. Christians ! tell me what is dearer to you than aught else in Christianity, so that I may in this matter direct your efforts." He stopped and waited. In the temple a dull echo arose. The members of the council whispered among themselves. Pope Peter, passionately gesticulating, was explaining something to those about him. Professor Pauli shook his head and smacked his lips with exasperation. The venerable John, bending over the Eastern bishops and monks, was quietly suggesting something to them. Having waited several minutes, the Emperor turned to the council and, with the same caressing tone, in which nevertheless there sounded a scarcely perceptible note of irony, said : " Dear Christians, I understand how difficult it is for you to give a direct answer. I desire to aid you in this matter. You, from time immemorial, unhappily have been so divided into various sects and parties that you have not perhaps a common object to which you are all attached. But if you are not able to agree among yourselves, then I hope to bring all parties into agreement, as I shall show to them all the same love and the same readiness to satisfy the *true* aspirations of each. Dear Christians, I know that for many, and not the meanest of you, the thing that is dearer than aught else in Christianity is that *spiritual authority* which it gives to its lawful representatives, not for their own profit, of course, but for the common good, since upon this authority is founded a regular spiritual order and moral discipline indispensable to all. Dear brother Catholics ! O, how I understand your point of view, and how I should like to rest my empire on the authority of your spiritual head ! In order that you should not think that this is flattery and empty phrases, we solemnly declare that it is agreeable to our autocratic will that the supreme bishop of all Catholics, the Pope of Rome, shall now ascend his throne in Rome with all the former rights and privileges of his position and chair, whensoever granted by our predecessors, beginning with the Emperor Constantine the Great. And from you, brother Catholics, I desire, in return for this, only a true and heartfelt acknowledgment of myself as your sole protector and defender. If there is anyone here who acknowledges me as such in his heart and in his conscience, let him come hither to me." And he pointed to the empty places on the daïs. With joyful shouts of *"Gratias agimus Domine! Salvum fac magnum imperatorem"* almost all the princes of the Catholic Church, the cardinals and bishops, a great part of the believing laymen, and more than half of the monks ascended the daïs, and, after making low bows in the direction of the Emperor, took their places. But below in the middle of the assembly, erect and immovable as a marble statue, sat in his place the Pope, Peter II. All who had surrounded him were on the dais. But the thinned ranks of monks and laymen which were left below closed around him, forming a tight ring, from whence was heard suppressed whispering: *" Non prævalebunt, non prævalebunt portæ inferni."*

Glancing in amazement at the motionless Pope, the Emperor again raised his voice: " Dear brethren, I know there are among you those to whom the holy tradition of Christianity, with its old symbols, hymns and prayers, icons and divine ritual is dearer than aught else. What, indeed, can be dearer than this to the devout soul? Know, then, that to-day a decree has been signed by me and large sums allotted for a universal museum of Christian archæology in our glorious imperial city of Constantinople for the purpose of collecting, studying and preserving all the monuments of ecclesiastical antiquity, preferably those of the East; and I further ask you to choose to-morrow from amongst yourselves a committee to consider with me those measures which it is necessary to take for the possible approximation of the traditions and institutions of the holy Orthodox Church to modern conditions, morals and customs. Brothers of the Orthodox faith, you who have my wishes at heart, who feel in your hearts that you can call me your true guide and lord, come up hither." A large part of the hierarchy of the East and North, half of the former Old Believers and more than half of the Orthodox priests, monks and laymen with joyful cries ascended the daïs, glancing proudly at the Catholics who were seated there. But the venerable John did not move and gave a deep sigh. And when the crowd round him were greatly thinned, he left his bench and seated himself nearer to Pope Peter and his circle. After him followed the others who had not gone upon the daïs. Again the Emperor began to speak. " I know there are some of you dear Christians to whom the personal assurance of truth and free investigation of the Scriptures is of all things the dearest in Christianity. I think there is no need to expatiate upon the matter.

Possibly you know that in my early youth I wrote a long treatise on Biblical criticism, which made at the time a certain sensation and was the foundation upon which my reputation was built. Probably, in recognition of this, the university of Tubingen has sent me, at this time, a request to accept from it the honorary diploma of Doctor of Theology. I commanded an answer to be given that I accepted it with pleasure and gratitude. And to-day, in addition to the museum of Christian archæology, I have allotted 1,500,000 marks from the yearly budget for the foundation of a universal institute for the free investigation of the Holy Scriptures from all possible points of view and in all possible directions and for instruction in all allied sciences. If there are any of you to whom my sincere goodwill is pleasing and who are able honestly to acknowledge me as their sovereign leader, I ask them to come hither to the new Doctor of Theology;" and a strange smile passed lightly over the beautiful lips of the great man. More than half of the learned theologians moved, though with a certain hesitation and wavering, towards the daïs. All looked round at Professor Pauli, who remained as if rooted to his seat. The learned theologians who had ascended the daïs were filled with confusion, and suddenly one, waving his hand, leapt straight down past the steps and ran to Professor Pauli and the minority which remained beside him. The latter raised his head, and rising with a somewhat vague movement, went past the empty benches, accompanied by his co-believers who had resisted, and sat down with them near the venerable John and Pope Peter and their circle.

The great majority of the council, among which were included almost all the hierarchy of the East and West, found themselves on the daïs. Below there remained only three groups, who were coming together and pressing about John, Pope Peter and Professor Pauli.

The Emperor turned to them and said in a sad tone: " What more can I do for you ? Strange people ! What do you want of me ? I know not. You yourselves, who are forsaken by the majority of your brethren and leaders and are condemned by popular sentiment, tell me what is dearer to you than aught else in Christianity ? " Then, like a white taper, the venerable John arose and gently answered : " For us the dearest thing of all in Christianity is Christ Himself—He alone, all is from Him, for we know that in Him dwells all the fulness of the Godhead in the flesh. From thee, sire, we are ready to accept every good thing, if only in thy generous hand we recognise the holy hand of Christ. And to thy question : ' What art thou able to do for us ? '—here is our answer : ' Confess now before us, Jesus Christ, the Son of God, Who came in the flesh, Who rose from the dead, and Who will come again. Confess Him, and we, with love will receive you as the true forerunner of His glorious coming.' " He was silent and fixed his eyes on the face of the Emperor. Something untoward had happened to the latter. Within him arose a diabolical tempest, such as he had experienced on that fatal night. He completely lost

47

all inner equilibrium, and all his thoughts were concentrated upon preventing himself from being deprived of his external self-possession or from betraying himself inopportunely. He made a superhuman effort not to throw himself with wild howls upon the speaker, and tear him to pieces with his teeth. Suddenly he heard a known but unearthly voice : " Be silent and fear not." He kept silent. Only his face, which was dark and deathlike, became all distorted, and sparks flew from his eyes. Whilst John had been speaking the great magician, wrapped in his immense tri-coloured mantle, which covered the cardinal's crimson, seemed to be manipulating something under it ; his eyes flashed in deep concentration and his lips moved. Through the open windows of the temple an enormous black cloud could be seen coming, and it soon became dark. John did not turn his astonished and frightened eyes from the face of the Emperor, till suddenly he sprang back in horror, and looking round cried out in a stifled voice: " Little children, it is Antichrist." At this moment, simultaneously with a deafening clap of thunder a great flash of lightning enveloped the old man. For an instant all were stunned, and when the dazed Christians came to themselves, the venerable John lay dead.

The Emperor, pale but composed, turned to the council : " You have witnessed the judgment of God. I desired not the death of anyone, but my heavenly Father will avenge His well-beloved Son. The matter is decided. Who will contend against the Most High ? Secretaries, write : ' The General Council of All Christians, after fire from heaven destroyed the foolish opponent of divine majesty, unanimously recognise the autocratic Emperor of Rome and of all the World as its supreme guide and lord.'" Suddenly a loud and distinct word is heard throughout the temple : " *Contradicitur !* " Pope Peter II. arose, and with flushed face, trembling with anger, raised his staff in the direction of the Emperor. " Our only Lord is Jesus Christ, Son of the Living God. And thou hast heard who thou art. Away from us ! Cain, fratricide ! Away, instrument of the devil ! By the power of Christ, I, the servant of the servants of God, cast thee out for ever, abominable dog, from the city of God, and deliver thee up to thy father Satan. Anathema ! Anathema ! Anathema ! " While he was speaking the great magician moved uneasily under his mantle, and louder than the last anathema the thunder rumbled, and the last Pope fell lifeless. " Thus by the hand of my Father are all my enemies destroyed," said the Emperor. " *Pereant, pereant,*" cried the trembling princes of the Church. He turned and, leaning upon the shoulder of the great magician, accompanied by all the throng, went out slowly by a door behind the daïs. In the temple there remained the two dead bodies and the narrow circle of Christians, half dead with terror. The only one who was not confused was Professor Pauli. It was as if the general horror had aroused all the forces of his soul. He had changed outwardly, he had an exalted and inspired look. With a resolute step he ascended the daïs, and having taken a seat vacated by one of the secretaries of state, he took a sheet of paper and began to write something on it. Having finished, he got up and read out in a loud voice : " To the glory of our only Saviour, Jesus Christ. The General Council of God's Church, gathered together in Jerusalem, after our blessed brother John, representative of Eastern Christianity, had detected in the great deceiver and enemy of God the true Antichrist predicted in God's word, and after our blessed father, Peter, the representative of Western Christianity, had lawfully and rightfully consigned him to eternal separation from the Church of God ; now, before these two witnesses of Christ, who have been killed for the truth, we decide to break off relations with his cursed and abominable assembly, and to go into the wilderness, there to await the imminent coming of our true Lord, Jesus Christ." Animation filled the crowd, and loud cries broke forth : " *Adveniat! adveniat cito. Komm, Herr Jesu, komm!* Come, Lord Jesus ! "

Professor Pauli wrote and then read out : " Having adopted this first and last act of the last general council, we sign our names "—and he made a sign of invitation to the assembly. All went up on the platform and signed. At the end, in large Gothic script, was written—" *decorum defunctorum testium locum tenens, Ernst Pauli.*" " Now let us go with our ark of the last covenant," he said, pointing to the two who had died. The bodies were raised on stretchers. Slowly, with Latin chants, and with German and Slavonic hymns, the Christians set forth to the entrance of Kharam-esh-Sherif. Here the procession was stopped by a secretary of state sent by the Emperor and escorted by an officer, with a platoon of guards. The soldiers stopped at the entrance, and the secretary of state read out as follows from an elevated position : " The command of his divine majesty ! For the instruction of Christian people and to protect them against wickedly-disposed persons who are causing disturbances and seducing the people, we have recognised it is for the public good to exhibit publicly the bodies of the two agitators, killed by fire from heaven, in Christian Street (*Kharet-an-Nasara*), at the entrance of the great temple of that religion, named The Holy Sepulchre or The Resurrection, so that all may be persuaded of the reality of their death. Their obstinate adherents, wickedly refusing all our favours and madly closing their eyes to the obvious signs of divinity, have, by being obedient to those who were killed by fire from heaven, put themselves outside our mercy and protection in the face of the heavenly Father. They shall be given full freedom with the single prohibition, on account of the public weal, of not being allowed to live in cities or other inhabited places, so that they may not trouble or seduce innocent and simple-minded people with their evil inventions." When he had finished, eight soldiers at the command of the officer approached the stretchers bearing the bodies.

" What is written is being fulfilled," said Professor Pauli, and the Christians who bore the stretchers handed them over in silence to the soldiers, who withdrew through the north-west gates ; but the Christians, issuing from the north-east gates, hurriedly set out from the city, and, passing the Mount of Olives, went towards Jericho, along a road which previously had been cleared of the mob by *gendarmes* and two cavalry regiments. On the barren hills near Jericho it was decided to wait for a few days. The following morning Christian pilgrims arrived from Jerusalem and related what had taken place in Zion. After the court dinner, all the members of the assembly were invited to the great throne room (near the supposed place of Solomon's throne), and the Emperor, turning to the representatives of the Catholic hierarchy, declared that the welfare of the Church evidently demanded from them a speedy choice of a worthy successor of the Apostle Peter ; that, according to the circumstances of the time, the election would have to be summary ; that the presence of himself, the Emperor, as leader and representative of the whole Christian world, abundantly made up for any omissions of ritual ; and that he, in the name of all Christians, proposed that the Sacred College should elect his well-beloved friend and brother Apollyon, thus making the close bond a lasting one and the union between the Church and the empire indissoluble for their common good. The Sacred College withdrew to a special apartment for the conclave, and returned in half an hour with the new Pope Apollyon. Whilst the balloting was taking place, the Emperor gently, wisely and eloquently persuaded the Orthodox and Evangelical representatives, in view of the great new era of Christian history, to put an end to their divisions, trusting to his word that Apollyon would be able to abolish for ever all the historical abuses of the papal power. Persuaded by this speech, the representatives of Orthodoxy and Protestantism drew up an Act for the union of the Churches, and when Apollyon, accompanied by the cardinals, appeared in the throne room, amidst the joyful cries of the whole assembly, a Greek bishop and an evangelical pastor tendered him their document. *"Accipio et approbo et lætificatur cor meum,"* said Apollyon, signing the paper. " I am as truly Orthodox and Evangelical as I am Catholic," he added, and affectionately exchanged kisses with the Greek and the German. Afterwards he went to the Emperor, who embraced him and held him a long time in his arms. At this time some shining spots began to float about the palace and the temple in all directions ; they grew and changed into bright forms of strange things ; flowers unseen upon earth showered down from above, filling the air with an unknown perfume. From on high resounded ravishing sounds of musical instruments, unheard up to that time, which went straight to the soul and transported the heart, and the angelic voices of an invisible choir sang the praises of the new lord of heaven and earth. Meanwhile a strange subterranean rumbling was heard in the north-west corner of the middle palace under *kubet-el-aruakh— i.e., kupolom dush,* where, according to Mussulman tradition, was the entrance into hell. When the assembly, by invitation of the Emperor, moved in that direction, all clearly heard innumerable high and piercing voices—not childish, not devilish— which were crying out " The time has come, release

53

us, our saviours." But when Apollyon, pressing close against the wall, cried out something three times in an unknown tongue, the voices were silent and the rumbling ceased. Meanwhile an enormous multitude of people from all quarters had surrounded Kharam-esh-Sherif. At the approach of night the Emperor, together with the new Pope, went out on the eastern staircase, where his presence aroused a storm of enthusiasm. He bowed affably on all sides, and then Apollyon, from a large basket brought to him by the cardinal deacons, repeatedly took and threw into the air magnificent roman candles, rockets and fountains of fire, which had been set alight by contact with his hand, and which were sometimes pearly phosphorescent, sometimes all the colours of the rainbow. And all of them, when they reached the earth, changed into numberless parti-coloured leaves with full and unconditional indulgences for all sins, past, present and to come. The popular joy passed all bounds. It is true that certain people affirmed that they saw with their own eyes the indulgences change into most repulsive toads and serpents. Nevertheless, the vast majority was in ecstasies and the popular festival continued for several days, during which time the new wonder-working Pope attained to things so wonderful and improbable that to mention them would be altogether useless. Meanwhile on the deserted heights of Jericho, the Christians gave themselves up to prayer and fasting. On the evening of the fourth day as it became dark, Professor Pauli and ten companions, mounted on asses and taking with them a cart, stole into Jerusalem and through side streets past Kharam-esh-Sherif, came out on Kharet-en-Nasar and approached the entrance to the Church of the Resurrection, where on the pavement lay the bodies of Pope Peter and the venerable John. The street at this hour was empty, everybody had gone to Kharam-esh-Sherif. The soldiers on guard had fallen into a deep sleep. Those who came for the bodies found them entirely untouched by corruption, and not even stiff or heavy. Having raised them upon the stretchers and having covered them with the mantles they had brought, they returned by the same roundabout way to their own people, but scarcely had they lowered the stretchers on the ground than the spirit of life entered into the dead. They moved and attempted to throw off the cloaks in which they were wrapped. All with joyful cries began to assist them, and both having come to life, stood up on their feet, whole and sound. And the venerable John began to speak: " So, little children, we have not parted, and now I say to you, it is time to carry out Christ's last prayer about His followers, that they should be one even as He with the Father is one. So for the sake of this unity of Christ we revere, little children, our well-beloved brother, Peter. May he feed the last of Christ's sheep." And he embraced Peter. Then Professor Pauli went up to him. *" Tu est Petrus,"* he said to the Pope, *" jetzt ist es ja gründlich erwiesen und ausser jedern Zweifel gesetzt."* He seized his hand firmly with his own right hand and gave his left to the venerable John with the words: *" So also, Väterchen, nun*

sind wir ja Eins in Christo." Thus was accomplished
the union of the churches in the darkness of the night
on a high and lonely place. But the darkness was
suddenly lightened by a bright splendour and there
appeared a great wonder in heaven : a woman clothed
in the sun with the moon under her feet and a
crown of twelve stars on her head. The apparition
remained for some time in one place and then moved
slowly towards the south. Pope Peter raised his
staff and cried out : " There is our banner, let us
follow it." And he went in the direction of the
vision, accompanied by both the old men and the
whole company of Christians, to the mountain of
of God—to Sinai.

(*Here the reader stopped.*)

LADY.—Why don't you continue ?

MR. Z.—The manuscript doesn't continue.
Father Pansophia did not succeed in finishing his
tale. When he was already ill he told me what more
he wished to write " when I am better." But he did
not get well, and the end of the tale was buried with
him in the Danilof monastery.

LADY.—But, of course, you remember what he
told you, so let us hear it.

MR. Z.—I remember only the principal features.
After the spiritual leaders and representatives of
Christianity withdrew to the Arabian desert, where
crowds of believers jealous for the truth flocked to
them from all countries, the new Pope was able,
without any obstacle, to pervert by his wonders and
prodigies all the superficial Christians who had not
been disillusioned by Antichrist, and who remained

56

with him. He declared that, by the power of the keys, he had opened the door between life on earth and life beyond the grave, and in fact, communication between the living and dead, and also between people and demons had been accomplished with the usual manifestations, and new unheard-of scenes of mystical debauchery and demonolatry took place. But scarcely had the Emperor begun to feel himself standing upon a firm religious foundation, and scarcely had he according to the persistent inspiration of his mysterious " father's " voice, declared himself the only true incarnation of supreme and universal Divinity, than a new misfortune fell upon him from an unexpected quarter : the revolt of the Hebrews. This nation, whose numbers at that time had reached thirty millions, was not entirely ignorant of the preparations for and the consolidation of the world-wide successes of the superman. When he moved to Jerusalem, secretly spreading the report in Hebrew circles that his principal problem was to establish the world-wide dominion of Israel, the Hebrews recognised him as the Messiah, and their enthusiastic devotion to him knew no bounds. But suddenly they rose in rebellion, breathing anger and vengeance. This revolution, undoubtedly predicted in the Scriptures and tradition, is set forth by Father Pansophia with, it may be, too much simplicity and realism. The trouble was, that the Hebrews, deeming the Emperor entirely Jewish by race, discovered by chance that he was not even circumcised. That very day Jerusalem, and the following day, all Palestine, was in revolt. The boundless and fervent devotion to the Saviour of Israel, to the promised Messiah, was changed into equally boundless and fervent hatred of the wily deceiver and brazen impostor. All Israel rose as one man, and its enemies saw with amazement that the soul of Israel, in its depths, lived not by calculations and the desires of Mammon, but by the force of a concentrated feeling—in the expectation of and passion for its eternal Messianic faith. The Emperor, who had not expected such an outbreak, at once lost his self-possession and issued an edict condemning to death all insubordinate Jews and Christians. Many thousands and tens of thousands who had not succeeded in arming themselves were slaughtered without mercy. But soon an army of a million Hebrews occupied Jerusalem, and locked up Antichrist in Kharam-esh-Sherif. He had at his disposal only a part of the guards, who were unable to overcome the masses of the enemy. By the help of the magic art of his Pope the Emperor succeeded in passing through the lines of his besiegers, and quickly appeared again in Syria with an innumerable army of pagans of different races. The Hebrews went forth to meet him with small hope of success. But hardly had the vanguard of both armies come together, when an earthquake of unprecedented violence occurred, the crater of an enormous volcano opened by the Dead Sea, about which lay the imperial army, and streams of fire flowed together in one flaming lake and swallowed up the Emperor himself and his numberless forces, together with Pope Apollyon, who always accompanied him, and for whom all his magic was of no avail. Meanwhile, the Hebrews hastened to Jerusalem in fear and trembling, calling for salvation to the God of Israel. When the holy city was already in sight, the heavens were rent by vivid lightning, from the east to the west, and they saw Christ coming towards them in royal apparel, and with the wounds from the nails in His outstretched hands. At the same time, from Sinai to Zion, went the company of Christians, led by Peter, John and Paul, and from various other parts hurried more triumphant multitudes : these consisted of all the Jews and Christians who had been killed by Antichrist. They lived and reigned with Christ for a thousand years. With this Father Pansophia wished to end his narrative, which had for its object, not a universal cataclysm of creation, but the conclusion of our historical process, which consists of the appearance, glorification and destruction of Antichrist.

POLITICIAN.—And do you think that this conclusion is so near ?

MR. Z.—Well, there will still be much chatter and fuss on the stage, but the whole drama is written to the end, and neither the actors nor the audience will be permitted to change anything in it.

LADY.—But what is the absolute meaning of this drama ? I still do not understand why Antichrist hates God so much, while he himself is essentially good, not evil.

MR. Z.—That's the point, he is not *essentially* so. All the meaning is in that. I take back my previous words that " you cannot explain Antichrist by

59

proverbs alone." He can be explained by a simple proverb, " All is not gold that glitters." You know this glitter of counterfeit good ; take it away and no real force remains—none.

GENERAL.—But you notice, too, upon what the curtain falls in this historical drama—upon war— the meeting of two armies. So the end of our conversation has come back to where it was at the beginning. How does this please you, Prince ? . . . Good heavens ! where's the Prince ?

POLITICIAN.—Didn't you see, then ? He went out quietly in that pathetic passage where the venerable John presses Antichrist to the wall. I did not wish to interrupt at the time, and afterwards I forgot.

GENERAL.—He has taken to flight, I swear it, and that's for the second time. He mastered himself the first time and came back. But this last was too much for him. Well ! Well !